Monetary Policy Lessons and the Way Ahead

March 23, 2015

Page Intentionally Left Blank

For over six years, the federal funds rate has, effectively, been zero. However it is widely expected that the rate will lift off before the end of this year, as the normalization of monetary policy gets underway.

The approach of liftoff reflects the significant progress we have made toward our objectives of maximum employment and price stability. The extraordinary monetary policy accommodation that the Federal Reserve has undertaken in response to the crisis has contributed importantly to the economic recovery, though the recovery has taken longer than we expected. The unemployment rate, at 5.5 percent in February, is nearing estimates of its natural rate, and we expect that inflation will gradually rise toward the Fed's target of 2 percent. Beginning the normalization of policy will be a significant step toward the restoration of the economy's normal dynamics, allowing monetary policy to respond to shocks without recourse to unconventional tools.

I would like to take this occasion to look back on some lessons learned during our time at the effective lower bound on the interest rate, and also to look forward.[1]

Monetary Policy since the Crisis

Let me first take a step back in time. Prior to the crisis, the financial system was more fragile than we realized. Key vulnerabilities included excessive leverage, overdependence on short-term funding, and deficiencies in credit ratings, underwriting standards, and risk management. Importantly, interconnections across financial institutions heightened the risk of contagion through cascading losses. Some of these interconnections emerged from the use of complicated financial instruments that created seemingly safe and liquid assets. At the time, it was common to say that risk was being

---

[1] The views that I offer are my own and not necessarily those of any other member of the Federal Open Market Committee or of the Committee itself.

dispersed and allocated to those best able to bear it. But rather than distributing risk widely, these instruments concentrated risk on the balance sheets of a relatively small number of highly levered financial institutions.

As a result, as the subprime crisis developed, market participants pulled back from risk taking, leading to deleveraging spirals and fire sales.[2] The damage spread across the globe. Following the collapse of Lehman Brothers on September 15, international trade collapsed as panic and financial connections transmitted distress across borders.[3] Of course, the economy's vulnerabilities did not stem from the private sector alone: in the public sector, gaps in the regulatory structure allowed important financial institutions to escape comprehensive supervision, and regulators were insufficiently focused on the stability of the system as a whole.

The Federal Reserve responded aggressively to the crisis.[4] By the end of 2008, the Federal Open Market Committee (FOMC) had reduced the target federal funds rate from 5-1/4 percent to, effectively, zero. The Fed also acted forcefully as the lender of last resort--in its traditional role of providing short-term liquidity to depository

---

[2] For a model in which fire sales can arise from uncertainty about the network of cross-exposures among banks, see Caballero and Simsek (2013).

[3] The fallout from the crisis was large even in countries that had not experienced an acute financial crisis. As an example, in six Asian countries, including China and India, exports fell more than 30 percent by the beginning of 2009, and industrial production declined about 10 percent. See the discussion of China, India, Indonesia, Malaysia, Thailand, and Taiwan in Coulibaly, Sapriza, and Zlate (2011). Regarding the role of credit conditions in the collapse of international trade, see Chor and Manova (2012).

[4] A key trigger for the crisis was the decline in housing prices, which began in 2006 and led to uncertainty about mortgage investments. In the summer of 2007, two large financial institutions--The Bear Stearns Companies, Inc., and BNP Paribas Group--suspended redemptions from certain investment funds, perhaps marking the beginning of the financial crisis. In 2008, the crisis intensified with the near collapse of Bear Stearns in March and the bankruptcy of Lehman Brothers Holdings in September; a full-scale financial panic ensued across much of the global financial system.

institutions, and also by providing liquidity directly to borrowers and investors in key credit markets.[5]

In addition, the worldwide scope of the crisis called for concerted international action. Because of the global nature of dollar funding markets, the Fed authorized dollar liquidity swap lines with major central banks, beginning in December 2007. In October 2008, central bankers coordinated reductions in policy rates and the Group of Seven agreed to use all available tools to prevent the failure of systemically important financial institutions.[6] The next month, the Group of Twenty announced a broad common strategy, including fiscal expansion.

These steps likely prevented a second Great Depression, but they were not sufficient to avoid a severe global contraction.

In the United States, with the federal funds rate at its effective lower bound by the end of 2008, the FOMC judged that it could not provide much additional accommodation via its conventional tool--reducing the federal funds rate.[7] Instead, the FOMC used two unconventional tools: large-scale asset purchases and enhanced forward guidance. To varying extents, foreign central banks have also been using these tools.

---

[5] In our role as lender of last resort, we worked closely with the Treasury Department and the Federal Deposit Insurance Corporation (FDIC). For example, to stem the run on money market funds, the Treasury provided a temporary guarantee and the Fed created a backstop liquidity program. In addition, the FDIC established the Temporary Liquidity Guarantee Program to guarantee certain unsecured liabilities of depository institutions and some bank holding companies.

[6] On October 8, 2008, the Federal Reserve and five other major central banks jointly announced a reduction in policy interest rates. See Bank of Canada and others (2008).

[7] A handful of central banks in Europe have recently set certain policy rates below zero. Specifically, the Danmarks Nationalbank, the European Central Bank, the Sveriges Riksbank, and the Swiss National Bank have set negative policy rates. In the United States, when the Federal Reserve sought to provide more accommodation despite the federal funds rate being, essentially, zero, we chose not to use negative rates, judging at the time that the small additional support for aggregate demand was not worth the accompanying risks to U.S. money markets and the intermediation of credit.

The Fed's asset purchases did not have the conventional aim of increasing reserve balances to pull down short-term rates.[8] Rather, purchases of longer-term securities lowered *longer-term yields* through portfolio balance effects.

The evolution of our asset purchases reflected a learning process for policymakers. In the early programs, the FOMC specified the expected quantities of assets to be acquired over a defined period. In contrast, with QE3 (the most recent round of quantitative easing, implemented from September 2012 to October 2014), the FOMC announced that we would continue to purchase securities at a certain monthly pace until the outlook for the labor market improved substantially in a context of price stability. Later, the FOMC noted that the pace of purchases was also data dependent, allowing the pace to be revised based on its assessment of progress toward its long-run objectives.

With the federal funds rate near zero and the Fed creating and adjusting new asset purchase programs, it became difficult for the public to anticipate how the FOMC would likely conduct monetary policy and respond to changing economic conditions. Thus, the FOMC began to rely heavily on enhanced forward guidance to communicate its intentions. Forward guidance works in part because it also constrains the flexibility of decisionmakers when the time comes to make their future decisions.[9]

---

[8] Indeed, the maturity extension program--also known as Operation Twist--did not increase reserves at all.
[9] There is a long literature in monetary economics about time inconsistency. Time inconsistency is the notion that, to achieve good outcomes, a central bank may need to make commitments about how it will act in the future--commitments that must be credible but that, ex post, the central bank might find hard to follow through on. For canonical papers, see Kydland and Prescott (1977) and Lucas and Stokey (1983); see also Fischer (1980). The early literature focused on the inability of central banks, in normal times, to commit to high future interest rates and low inflation. Interestingly, at the zero lower bound, central banks may face nearly the opposite commitment problem: To escape a liquidity trap, a central bank may want to commit to keep interest rates low and accommodate an output boom even after the headwinds from a crisis have dissipated. See, for example, Eggertsson (2006) and Werning (2012). For additional discussion of Federal Reserve communications, see Yellen (2012) and Stein (2014).

Nonetheless, a number of potential costs might be associated with unconventional tools. When interest rates are extremely low, risks to financial stability might grow. In addition, elevated securities holdings could reduce the Fed's income and remittances to the U.S. Treasury when rates eventually rise.[10]

Further, the Fed's quantitative easing appeared significantly to affect foreign asset markets, and to have contributed to a surge of capital inflows to emerging-market economies (EMEs).[11] Our asset purchase programs were even called a "currency war." However, eventually, most EMEs seemed glad to receive those flows. Interestingly, the asset purchases recently announced by the European Central Bank (ECB) appear to be putting downward pressure on *longer-term* interest rates in the United States. In addition, the ECB's policy should increase growth in Europe, which will be beneficial for U.S. exports. Although some of these benefits may be offset by the recent appreciation of the dollar, much of that increase likely reflects other factors including the relatively strong performance of the U.S. economy.

Looking back, there is ample evidence that supports the view that the Fed's asset purchases contributed to a stronger U.S. recovery, by raising the prices of the assets purchased and close substitutes, as well as those of riskier assets.[12] Our experience also

[10] For a discussion of the Federal Reserve's remittances, see Yellen (2013). Though it is likely that remittances to the Treasury will decline later in the decade as interest rates increase, such developments would not impair the Federal Reserve's conduct of monetary policy, and it is highly likely that average annual remittances over the period affected by our asset purchases will be higher than pre-crisis norms. In addition, the asset purchases also affect Treasury revenue by lifting economic activity and thereby tax revenue, as well as by lowering interest rates and thereby debt service costs.
[11] Regarding the effects on foreign asset markets, see Neely (2011); Fratzscher, Lo Duca, and Straub (2013); and Rogers, Scotti, and Wright (2014). Regarding the effects on EMEs, it appears that both conventional and unconventional policies in the United States--among other factors--have driven capital flows into EMEs. See, for example, Ahmed and Zlate (2014) and Bowman, Londono, and Sapriza (2014).
[12] See, for example, D'Amico and King (2013); Gagnon and others (2011); Gilchrist, López-Salido, and Zakrajšek (2014); and Hamilton and Wu (2012).

shows that forward guidance helped better align market expectations of Fed policy with the Committee's policy intentions.[13] In brief, unconventional policies helped bring down long-term yields both by reducing term premia and by lowering the expected path of future short-term rates.

The Recovery from the Financial Crisis

Despite monetary stimulus, the recovery from the financial crisis has been even more sluggish than we had expected. The slow recovery provides more evidence that severe financial crises have long-lived effects, as Reinhart and Rogoff, and others, have documented.[14]

The gradual pace of the recovery has likely reflected both demand and supply factors. With respect to aggregate demand, the economy faced several important headwinds: efforts by households and businesses to rebuild their balance sheets, persistently tight credit conditions, the extreme weakness of the housing sector, the significant drag from fiscal policy in the years from 2011 to 2013, and the growth slowdown in Europe and other parts of the world.

Turning to aggregate supply, it appears that productivity growth has slowed.[15] One notable manifestation of slow productivity growth is that last year, unemployment fell significantly further than we had anticipated as of the start of the year--a pattern that occurred in the prior four years as well--whereas gross domestic product growth fell short of our expectations, as it had in three of the four prior years. However, productivity is

---

[13] See, for example, Yellen (2011).

[14] See Cerra and Saxena (2008); Reinhart and Rogoff (2009); Schularick and Taylor (2012); Bordo and Haubrich (2012); and Howard, Martin, and Wilson (2011).

[15] The slowdown in productivity growth may predate the recession and may have been exacerbated by it. See Reifschneider, Wascher, and Wilcox (2013) and Fernald (2014).

extremely difficult to predict. For my part, I believe that the enormous gains in human welfare that the information technology explosion seems to be generating are likely to continue, and will perhaps eventually return measured productivity growth to its long-run historical pace.

Conditions for Liftoff

Although the recovery has been slow, there has been significant cumulative progress. An increase in the target federal funds range likely will be warranted before the end of the year. Liftoff should occur when the expected return from raising the interest rate outweighs the expected costs of doing so. In deciding when that time has come, we will continue to monitor a wide range of information regarding labor market conditions, inflation, and financial and international developments. We anticipate that it will be appropriate to raise the target range when there has been further improvement in the labor market and we are reasonably confident that inflation will move back to our 2 percent objective over the medium term.

Policy Normalization

Full normalization of monetary policy would allow the Fed to rely on its traditional policy framework of adjustments to the federal funds rate. However, as long as our balance sheet remains sizable, we will not be able to implement monetary policy with our traditional tool of repurchases. It is important that, when we change the rate for the first time in a long time, we are certain that we have the operational tools to control the federal funds rate—and, accordingly, we have developed and tested new operational tools to control the federal funds rate.

As discussed in the FOMC's statement titled Policy Normalization Principles and Plans, which was published following the September 2014 FOMC meeting, we will use the rate of interest on excess reserves (IOER) as our primary tool to control the federal funds rate.[16] We also plan to use an overnight reverse repurchase agreement (ON RRP) facility, as needed. In an ON RRP operation, counterparties may invest funds with the Fed at a given rate, possibly subject to a cap on the aggregate amount invested. Because ON RRP counterparties include many money market participants that are not eligible to receive IOER, the facility can be a powerful tool for controlling money market interest rates. Indeed, testing to date by the New York Fed suggests that ON RRP operations have generally established a soft floor for such rates.[17]

However, an ON RRP program also has certain risks. For example, a large and persistent program could have unanticipated and adverse effects on the structure of money markets. In addition, in times of stress, demand for the safety and liquidity of ON RRPs with the central bank might increase sharply, potentially exacerbating disruptive flight-to-quality flows.[18] To mitigate these risks, the FOMC has agreed that it will use an ON RRP facility only to the extent necessary and will phase it out when it is no longer needed.

In addition, the Fed has been discussing and testing other supplementary tools, such as term reverse repurchase agreements and term deposits, and can use these tools as needed to help support money market rates.

---

[16] See Board of Governors (2014a).

[17] Policymakers have discussed the benefits and costs of an ON RRP facility. For further discussion on this topic, see, for example, the FOMC minutes for June 2014, July 2014, and January 2015; see Board of Governors (2014b, 2014c, 2015).

[18] See Frost and others (2015). As the authors note, an ON RRP facility can also potentially contribute to financial stability by crowding out risky short-term borrowing by financial institutions and businesses.

With regard to balance sheet normalization, the FOMC has indicated that it does not anticipate selling agency mortgage-backed securities. When the time comes, we plan to normalize the balance sheet primarily by ceasing reinvestment of principal payments on existing holdings. When the FOMC chooses to cease reinvestments, the balance sheet will naturally contract, with a corresponding reduction in reserve balances. This runoff of our securities holdings will also gradually remove accommodation, an effect that we will need to take into account in setting the stance of policy.

During normalization, we will, no doubt, learn more about our different tools and make adjustments to our operating framework. In part because of this adaptability, I am confident that by using IOER and, as needed, these supplementary tools, we will be able to raise short-term interest rates when it becomes appropriate.

Monetary Policy after Liftoff

The focus of the great bulk of the discussion on monetary policy during the last few years, has been on liftoff--on the circumstances under which the FOMC will choose to raise the federal funds rate, on the date on which that will happen, and on the effect of the Fed's very large portfolio on how it will manage the liftoff process. Those questions are natural after more than six years during which the federal funds rate has been held at its effective lower bound.

But as liftoff approaches, we need to think also about what will happen next. For liftoff is only the start of the process of normalization, and, going forward, the FOMC will once again be changing the federal funds rate as necessary, both up and down. Accordingly, discussion of monetary policy needs to begin to shift to the future path of interest rates, and thus to the basis on which the FOMC will set interest rates following liftoff.

There has been a lively discussion of one element of the future path of the federal funds rate: whether liftoff should be sooner with a gradual rise in the rate, or whether liftoff should occur later and be followed by a steeper path of the rate.[19] These discussions are useful when considering the appropriate timing of the first increase in the federal funds rate. But what comes after the first increase? Standard interest rate projections might incline one to believe that the path of the federal funds rate after liftoff will consist of a steady rate of increase from zero to the longer-run normal nominal federal funds rate, which will be equal to the natural real rate of interest plus our 2 percent inflation goal. One might even look back to the period from 2004 to 2007 and conclude that the FOMC will raise the federal funds rate by 25 basis points every meeting, or every second meeting, or every third meeting, depending on the date of liftoff.

I know of no plans for the FOMC to behave that way. Why not? Isn't that what the calculation of optimal control paths shows? Yes. But a smooth path upward in the federal funds rate will almost certainly not be realized, because, inevitably, the economy will encounter shocks--shocks like the unexpected decline in the price of oil, or geopolitical developments that may have major budgetary and confidence implications, or a burst of greater productivity growth, as the Fed dealt with in the mid-1990s.

---

[19] For a discussion of the tradeoffs between the risks that would be associated with departing either earlier or later from the effective lower bound, see, for example, the FOMC minutes for January 2015; see Board of Governors (2015).

When shocks happen, as they do, policymakers will have to respond to at least some of them. Accordingly there is considerable uncertainty about the level of future interest rates--a degree of uncertainty that can be estimated statistically, and that should be taken into account by market participants and recognized by the FOMC when it discusses future levels of interest rates. The uncertainty about future levels of the federal funds rate can be represented in a "fan chart"--that is, a figure showing the expected path of the federal funds rate as well as a range representing the degree of uncertainty around that path.[20]

The two sure elements of forward guidance that the FOMC will be able to offer after liftoff are that monetary policy will continue to be aimed at fostering the Committee's dual objectives, and that it will be data driven. As we move away from the zero lower bound, the data to which we will be responding will be driven less and less by the financial crisis and Great Recession, and increasingly by post-liftoff economic developments. Whatever the state of the economy, the federal funds rate will be set at each FOMC meeting on the basis of what the members of the FOMC believe will best enable us to meet our dual goals of maximum employment and price stability over the course of time.

As the FOMC responds to incoming information, it will continue to be absolutely transparent in explaining its decisions and how and why they contribute to meeting the legally mandated dual goals of monetary policy. That transparency serves three purposes: First, it is required if we are to be accountable to the public; second, it is the

---

[20] For example, the Sveriges Riksbank publishes a fan chart that displays a forecast for its policy repurchase agreement (or repo) rate, along with uncertainty bands based on historical forecast errors, showing the ranges in which the repo rate is forecast to fall with 50 percent, 75 percent, and 90 percent confidence. For the chart, see Sveriges Riksbank (2015).

best way of ensuring that monetary policy decisionmakers continue to follow sensible and rational policies; and third, it is the best way of informing the private sector of the basis on which monetary policy decisions are made and will continue to be made.

With respect to forward guidance: its role has been and continues to be important in the long period in which eventual liftoff has been the key interest rate decision confronting the FOMC and the focus of market expectations. However, as monetary policy is normalized, interest rates will sometimes have to be increased, and sometimes decreased. Market participants will be able to form their expectations of future interest rates on the basis of three elements: first, the policy record of the FOMC, which might be approximated as a reaction function; second, their analysis of the current economic and financial situation and outlook; and, third, whatever guidance the FOMC will provide as to how it sees monetary policy decisions likely to unfold given the economic situation and outlook. It is likely that explicit long-term forward guidance will play less of a role in monetary policy after liftoff than it has during the past few years.

Policymakers' behavior is sometimes summarized as a reaction function, which can be an algebraic description of how the interest rate is set--for instance, a Taylor-type rule in which the federal funds rate reacts simultaneously to the rate of inflation and expectations of inflation as well as to the rate of unemployment and expected changes in the level of unemployment.[21] However, a simple rule of that sort will, by necessity, leave out many factors that appropriately influence monetary policy, such as financial developments, temporary divergences in relationships between different measures of

---

[21] Svensson (1997) notes that the reaction function might take the form of a "targeting rule" expressing how the policymaker's target variables are expected to move over time. Bernanke (2010) discusses the practical importance of targeting forecast, as opposed to realized, variables.

economic activity or inflation, and the like. A simple rule can provide the starting point for the decisions made by the FOMC, but in reaching their interest rate decision, members of the Committee will always have to use their judgment to identify the special circumstances confronting the economy, and how to react to them.

To ensure that monetary policy operates in as stabilizing a way as possible, the FOMC will continue to set out, as clearly as it can, the basis of every decision that it makes, and to provide guidance on its expectations of future decisions. And on the basis of the information provided by the FOMC, of their understanding of the historical record of Fed policy decisions, and of their analysis and expectations of the state of the economy and, particularly, the financial markets, market participants will make the best decisions they can.

References

Ahmed, Shaghil, and Andrei Zlate (2014). "Capital Flows to Emerging Market Economies: A Brave New World?" *Journal of International Money and Finance*, vol. 48 (November), pp. 221-48.

Bank of Canada, Bank of England, Board of Governors of the Federal Reserve System, European Central Bank, Sveriges Riksbank, and Swiss National Bank (2008). "FOMC Statement: Federal Reserve and Other Central Banks Announce Reductions in Policy Interest Rates," press release, October 8, www.federalreserve.gov/newsevents/press/monetary/20081008a.htm.

Bernanke, Ben S. (2010). "Monetary Policy and the Housing Bubble," speech delivered at the Annual Meeting of the American Economic Association, Atlanta, January 3, www.federalreserve.gov/newsevents/speech/bernanke20100103a.htm.

Board of Governors of the Federal Reserve System (2014a). "Federal Reserve Issues FOMC Statement on Policy Normalization Principles and Plans," press release, September 17, www.federalreserve.gov/newsevents/press/monetary/20140917c.htm.

------ (2014b). "Minutes of the Federal Open Market Committee, June 17-18, 2014," press release, July 9, www.federalreserve.gov/newsevents/press/monetary/20140709a.htm.

------ (2014c). "Minutes of the Federal Open Market Committee, July 29-30, 2014," press release, August 20, www.federalreserve.gov/newsevents/press/monetary/20140820a.htm.

------ (2015). "Minutes of the Federal Open Market Committee, January 27-28, 2015," press release, February 18, www.federalreserve.gov/newsevents/press/monetary/20150218a.htm.

Bordo, Michael D., and Joseph G. Haubrich (2012). "Deep Recessions, Fast Recoveries, and Financial Crises: Evidence from the American Record," Working Paper 12-14. Cleveland: Federal Reserve Bank of Cleveland, June, www.clevelandfed.org/~/media/Files/Working%20Papers/wp2012/wp1214-deep-recessions-fast-recoveries-and-financial-crisis-evidence-from-the-american-record.pdf.

Bowman, David, Juan M. Londono, and Horacio Sapriza (2014). "U.S. Unconventional Monetary Policy and Transmission to Emerging Market Economies," International Finance Discussion Papers 1109. Washington: Board of Governors of the Federal Reserve System, June, www.federalreserve.gov/pubs/ifdp/2014/1109/ifdp1109.pdf.

Caballero, Ricardo J., and Alp Simsek (2013). "Fire Sales in a Model of Complexity," *Journal of Finance*, vol. 68 (December), pp. 2549-87.

Cerra, Valerie, and Sweta Chaman Saxena (2008). "Growth Dynamics: The Myth of Economic Recovery," *American Economic Review*, vol. 98 (March), pp. 439-57.

Chor, Davin, and Kalina Manova (2012). "Off the Cliff and Back? Credit Conditions and International Trade during the Global Financial Crisis," *Journal of International Economics*, vol. 87 (May), pp. 117-33.

Coulibaly, Brahima, Horacio Sapriza, and Andrei Zlate (2011). "Trade Credit and International Trade during the 2008-09 Global Financial Crisis," International Finance Discussion Papers 1020. Washington: Board of Governors of the Federal Reserve System, June, www.federalreserve.gov/pubs/ifdp/2011/1020/ifdp1020.pdf.

D'Amico, Stefania, and Thomas B. King (2013). "Flow and Stock Effects of Large-Scale Treasury Purchases: Evidence on the Importance of Local Supply," *Journal of Financial Economics,* vol. 108 (May), pp. 425-48.

Eggertsson, Gauti B. (2006). "The Deflation Bias and Committing to Being Irresponsible," *Journal of Money, Credit and Banking,* vol. 38 (March), pp. 283-321.

Engen, Eric, Thomas Laubach, and David Reifschneider (2015). "The Macroeconomic Effects of the Federal Reserve's Unconventional Monetary Policies," Finance and Economics Discussion Series 2015-005. Washington: Board of Governors of the Federal Reserve System, January, www.federalreserve.gov/econresdata/feds/2015/files/2015005pap.pdf.

Fernald, John (2014). "Productivity and Potential Output before, during, and after the Great Recession," Working Paper Series 2014-15. San Francisco: Federal Reserve Bank of San Francisco, June, www.frbsf.org/economic-research/publications/working-papers/wp2014-15.pdf.

Fischer, Stanley (1980). "Dynamic Inconsistency, Cooperation and the Benevolent Dissembling Government," *Journal of Economic Dynamics and Control,* vol. 2 (February), pp. 93-107.

Fratzscher, Marcel, Marco Lo Duca, and Roland Straub (2013). "On the International Spillovers of U.S. Quantitative Easing," Working Paper Series 1557. Frankfurt: European Central Bank, June, www.ecb.europa.eu/pub/pdf/scpwps/ecbwp1557.pdf.

Frost, Josh, Lorie Logan, Antoine Martin, Patrick McCabe, Fabio Natalucci, and Julie Remache (2015). "Overnight RRP Operations as a Monetary Policy Tool: Some Design Considerations," Finance and Economics Discussion Series 2015-010.

Washington: Board of Governors of the Federal Reserve System, February, www.federalreserve.gov/econresdata/feds/2015/files/2015010pap.pdf.

Gagnon, Joseph, Matthew Raskin, Julie Remache, and Brian Sack (2011). "Large-Scale Asset Purchases by the Federal Reserve: Did They Work?" Federal Reserve Bank of New York, *Economic Policy Review,* vol. 17 (May), pp. 41-59, www.newyorkfed.org/research/staff_reports/sr441.html.

Gilchrist, Simon, David López-Salido, and Egon Zakrajšek (2014). "Monetary Policy and Real Borrowing Costs at the Zero Lower Bound," NBER Working Paper Series 20094. Cambridge, Mass.: National Bureau of Economic Research, May.

Hamilton, James D., and Jing Cynthia Wu (2012). "The Effectiveness of Alternative Monetary Policy Tools in a Zero Lower Bound Environment," *Journal of Money, Credit and Banking,* vol. 44 (February), pp. 3-46.

Howard, Greg, Robert Martin, and Beth Anne Wilson (2011). "Are Recoveries from Banking and Financial Crises Really So Different?" International Finance Discussion Papers 1037. Washington: Board of Governors of the Federal Reserve System, November, www.federalreserve.gov/Pubs/ifdp/2011/1037/ifdp1037.pdf.

Kydland, Finn E., and Edward C. Prescott (1977). "Rules Rather Than Discretion: The Inconsistency of Optimal Plans," *The Journal of Political Economy*, vol. 85 (June), pp. 473-91.

Lucas, Robert E., and Nancy L. Stokey (1983). "Optimal Fiscal and Monetary Policy in an Economy without Capital," *Journal of Monetary Economics*, vol. 12 (1), pp. 55-93.

Neely, Christopher J. (2011). "The Large-Scale Asset Purchases Had Large International Effects," Working Paper Series 2010-018C. St. Louis: Federal Reserve Bank of St. Louis, January, http://research.stlouisfed.org/conferences/qe/Neely_--_2010-018_1_.pdf.

Reifschneider, Dave, William Wascher, and David Wilcox (2013). "Aggregate Supply in the United States: Recent Developments and Implications for the Conduct of Monetary Policy," Finance and Economics Discussion Series 2013-77. Washington: Board of Governors of the Federal Reserve System, November, www.federalreserve.gov/pubs/feds/2013/201377/201377pap.pdf.

Reinhart, Carmen M., and Kenneth S. Rogoff (2009). "The Aftermath of Financial Crises," NBER Working Paper Series 14656. Cambridge, Mass.: National Bureau of Economic Research, January.

Rogers, John H., Chiara Scotti, and Jonathan H. Wright (2014). "Evaluating Asset-Market Effects of Unconventional Monetary Policy: A Cross-Country

Comparison," International Finance Discussion Papers 1101. Washington: Board of Governors of the Federal Reserve System, March, www.federalreserve.gov/pubs/ifdp/2014/1101/ifdp1101.pdf.

Schularick, Moritz, and Alan M. Taylor (2012). "Credit Booms Gone Bust: Monetary Policy, Leverage Cycles, and Financial Crises, 1870-2008," *American Economic Review*, vol. 102 (April), pp. 1029-61.

Stein, Jeremy C. (2014). "Challenges for Monetary Policy Communication," speech delivered at the Money Marketeers of New York University, New York, May 6, www.federalreserve.gov/newsevents/speech/stein20140506a.htm.

Svensson, Lares E.O. (1997). "Inflation Forecast Targeting: Implementing and Monitoring Inflation Targets," *European Economic Review*, vol. 41 (June), pp. 1111-46.

Sveriges Riksbank (2015). "Current Forecast for the Repo Rate, Inflation and GDP," webpage, February 12, figure ("Repo Rate with Uncertainty Bands"), www.riksbank.se/en/Monetary-policy/Forecasts-and-interest-rate-decisions/Current-forecast-for-the-repo-rate-inflation-and-GDP/.

Werning, Iván (2012). "Managing a Liquidity Trap: Monetary and Fiscal Policy," unpublished paper, Massachusetts Institute of Technology, March, http://economics.mit.edu/files/7558.

Yellen, Janet (2011). "Unconventional Monetary Policy and Central Bank Communications," speech delivered at the University of Chicago Booth School of Business U.S. Monetary Policy Forum, New York, New York, February 25, http://www.federalreserve.gov/newsevents/speech/yellen20110225a.htm

------. "Revolution and Evolution in Central Bank Communications," speech delivered at the University of California, Berkeley, Haas School of Business, Berkeley, Calif., November 13, www.federalreserve.gov/newsevents/speech/yellen20121113a.htm.

------ (2013). "Challenges Confronting Monetary Policy," speech delivered at the 2013 National Association for Business Economics Policy Conference, Washington, March 4, www.federalreserve.gov/newsevents/speech/yellen20130302a.htm.

www.ingramcontent.com/pod-product-compliance
Lightning Source LLC
Chambersburg PA
CBHW080632180526
45168CB00007B/3138